More Than I Could Ever Know

How I Survived Caregiving

by

Dale L. Baker

MsDale PUBLICATIONS
Peoria, Arizona

ISBN-13: 978-1496142894
ISBN-10: 1496142896

FIRST EDITION
MSDALE PUBLISHING™

For more information about permission to reproduce selections from this book, please contact the author at
msdalelbaker@gmail.com.

Book design by Rocky Berlier
Manufactured in the United States of America

CONTENTS

Continued...

DEDICATION

To all those who care for chronically ill loved ones. Welcome to my caregiver manual dedicated to hard-working heroes who take years off their own lives attempting to extend and enrich the lives of those they love.

ACKNOWLEDGMENTS

When I moved from Oregon to Arizona in 2012, this manuscript in its unorganized, infant form was one of the few things I brought with me. Since 2006, aspiring and published writers in critique groups in two states have helped me work through these episodes. I wish to acknowledge that audience and thank each member for pushing me forward, continually complimenting my ability and confirming the value of my message. This book has been, for the most part, a surprising delight to polish and publish in 2014. The passage of time has allowed me to revisit these memories with fewer tears and better editing.

I was fortunate to come across Rocky Berlier of *Concierge-Publishing.com* in my search for professional input. Thank you, Rocky, for finessing me into smoothing down the rough edges, filling in the voids and drawing clarity out of me when my words rambled on in lyrical lines that made little sense.

As for thanking those who saved my caregiver life, my caregiver support group at Providence Medical Center is right up there at the top. Confidentiality prevents me from naming names, but thank you guys for sharing and sobbing with me. We all know how much our times together meant to each and every one of us.

Second on the list would be Jeff Lindsey. You'll read about him in one of the last chapters. Thank you, Jeff, for being Rich's friend. I thank my sister Mary Reichley and her husband Darryl for coming to my rescue in Rich's final days and my neighbor Siu Ling Wong Ao for claiming me as a "sister."

Lastly, thank you, Richard William Baker for sharing twenty-nine years of your life with me. The last five were dicey, but you were worth it. Thank you, Sweetheart, for loving me even on my worst days, of which there were more than a few.

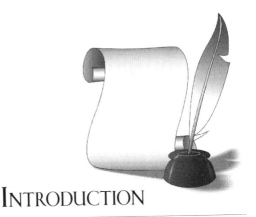

INTRODUCTION

I wrote most of this book during my hardest caregiving years (2005-2008). Some of it first appeared on my blog or a website I maintained in 2008. In reflection, now that half a decade has passed and my life has assumed a healthy glow, there seems to be a lot of whining in these stories. At the time, I was emptying my soul to future kindred spirits who were likewise seeking enlightenment for this job we didn't apply for. How quickly I have forgotten how lost and emotionally raw I felt.

In 2005 when I started offering early-written pages of this book to other writers for comment I was told I was writing a love story. There is a lot of love in this story. But I have more to share about bigger issues.

There is no easy way to love while pulling away. Yet that's what caregiver survival requires. Learning to be a whole instead of a half. Evaluating the intimate boundaries of devotion. Deciding the limits of responsibility to a loved one in the involuntary process of leaving us.

Caregiving leaves its mark on us. No matter what we do to prepare ourselves the hole left behind looms large.

I have plugged along, organizing these episodes into book format, thinking that they still have merit to some isolated, overwhelmed caregivers who do not have established networks of friends and legions of family to keep them from going insane or worse.

Caregivers are an underappreciated, overstressed bunch. It would please me greatly if non-caregivers would read this book, feel our pain and treat us better. Chances are, if you have not yet experienced it, but live long enough, somewhere along the line you will meet caregiving face-to-face. This is my contribution to that awareness campaign.

I've saddled this book with a lot of goals. I want it to motivate caregivers and non-caregivers in addition to raising philosophical relationship questions. I've offered helpful hints and shared my love story sprinkled with desperation and a rant here and there. That's a tall order for a little book. Whatever it is you are seeking inside these pages, I hope you find it and more.

So Dale L. Baker

Chapter One

CAREGIVER CAROUSEL

aregivers know about "the carousel". On a lacquered pony, you ride up (good days) and you ride down (bad days) but the music never stops. There's no choreography. No graceful dismount. Friends, relatives, neighbors stand as spectators. Like neon ribbons their sympathetic faces smear, merge then reappear as you circle in and out of their line of sight. Ignorant. Inexperienced. They have no idea. They see no rotating platform. They cannot hear the notes; feel the rhythm.

Rich and I have been married for over twenty-five years. We share a common history, full of intriguing moments and laughable characters. I have loved him and his size 14 feet ever since I met him in 1979. He wore blue work shirts and pounded steel for a living. I needed two hands to wrap my fingers around his biceps then and they still wouldn't touch.

That's him sitting on the carousel's wooden bench; the kiddy seat. He's too weak to get up on a horse any more.

Sometimes, I sit with him. We hold hands and comment on the events of our shared world in a comfortable, if not weary, state of denial. Like when we sit in our deck chairs under the magnolia tree out back, complimenting each other on the excellent quality of our sweet basil and oregano. We go on "hummingbird watch" there, laughing at Red, our resident hummer as he chases interlopers around the abelia and over the butterfly bush. Or, like when I crawl into his (what used to be *our*) bed to spread my body up against his cold, blanket-wrapped limbs; too fragile for hugs and squeezes like in the old days. We treasure the closeness, the whispered tenderness.

Most of the time, though, I'm "up on the horse" by myself, jousting medical giants and manipulating all things mundane. "Advocate" has become my middle name. Although we still discuss medical treatment options together, I have become the drawer of pictures, the repeater of words, the "rephraser" of sentences. He suffers from the cloudiness of "chemo-brain". Every decision about food, clothing, and transportation, I make alone or with just-enough explanation to assure cooperation if not agreement. I've given up grasping for the brass ring.

There are no more cures. My sweetheart has become my little boy, on his way to becoming my baby.

On bad days, my carousel pony rides down. There are constipation or pain issues. Oblivious to food or surroundings, he sits for hours; claims he's reading. Attempts at normalcy end in crisis. The smell of restaurant food drives him to nausea. His parchment-like skin tears and bleeds as he brushes an unfamiliar wall. His left foot drags, too weak to make a step. On good days, he can drive himself to acupuncture treatment and come back with his old smile. I ride my pony high.

The emotional merry-go-round continues, spinning tighter circles, constricted by tempo, a constant din and… I cannot get off. Despite well-meaning bystanders, the calliope in their midst is playing for two. I pray for an end, a smooth landing for us both, although I can't imagine what that would be. Not until the music stops.

Chapter Two

YOUR DECISION TO SURVIVE

Caregiving is intimate. It made me fall in love with my husband all over again. I wanted to keep him forever. But there's the rub. The more I merged myself into his struggle with life, the greater my sense of loss, as I watched him lose that battle. His needs consumed me so completely that I lost myself. I became a different person, a person who had forgotten how to live.

There is a world of difference between short and long-term caregiving. We humans can tolerate and prevail in incredible conditions for short periods of time. We rise magnificently to the occasion. Prolonged adversity, however, requires stamina and strategy. Adding "terminal" to the already weighty load makes the going tougher. We can't live without hope.

That's what this book is about. How I learned to nurture myself as well as my loved one. How I became aware of my own stages of grief and worked through the isolation, anger and depression. It wasn't always pretty, but it worked for me. I made it.

No one writes funny or lighthearted things about caregiving. In 2004, the few books available were drab, written by people of the cloth with no hands-on experience or clinicians who approached caregiving with the warmth of a pair of shiny scissors. What I learned about taking care of my dying husband, I didn't find in any book. It came from failing until something worked and sharing those failures with other sobbing caregivers.

I felt like I was gasping for breath the last three years that I took care of Richard. At times I was on a merry-go-round with flashing neon lights and unexpected stops. It was a sadistic fantasyland. I was thrust into a leading role where the script changed without notice. The music kept playing on past my limits of endurance or understanding. And the illusion of our final show together, like a carrot outside my donkey grasp faded in and out of sight. When the end did come it was ugly like nothing I had imagined or read about on the Internet.

The good news is I survived caregiving. But I had to work at it. I had to reclaim my spirit from the bottom of the pool and force life back into it—not once but often. It kept slipping under the surface like the neglected shell that I had allowed it to become. You too can survive caregiving, if you want to. I guess that's the first question you need to ask yourself.

I'm a recovering caregiver. I've tossed the medication schedules and packed away my spray bottle of wound cleanser, but my head is bursting with things I want to share. Things no one ever told me about how to take care of a dying husband. Things I had to learn after trying everything else. Things I learned in isolation because there wasn't anyone else. Just me and Richard, and he wasn't in very good shape, although he did try so very hard to help.

I have hints on nausea and constipation control. I share the joy of support groups, yoga, and widow's lists as well as the pitfalls of hospice selection and respite care. Learn about abusive patients, medicating the caregiver, making a lifeline list and dealing with end-of-life decisions. I have five years of material. I thought the last three years were going to kill me, but they didn't.

I don't want caregiving to kill you, either. But if you don't work at your own survival, long-term caregiving can take you under.

Taking care of Richard educated me beyond my naïve expectations, taught me invaluable hands-on coping skills that I wish I'd had at the beginning of my caregiving days. I truly hoped that I would *never* need to call again upon this wealth of knowledge to direct and comfort me but then my parents, one with Alzheimer's and the other with three-pages of typed medical history plus attitude, became a part of my daily life.

I suspect you are reading this because you are a seasoned caregiver, stuck in a duty-bound routine that long ago lost its sense of purpose. But perhaps, you are just starting your journey. Maybe you have just come from the doctor's office with a piece of paper placed in your hand, referring you and your loved one to what you may fear will be an ugly trail to the end of life. You face the entrance of an unknown labyrinth together. You are fearful and worry that if anyone emerges from the exit, it will be only you. You dread the journey. You doubt your abilities. You can't imagine what your short or long-term future will be.

In the pages that follow, I will share some of my caregiving days with you. We will cry together. My stories will be either lightweight or horrific compared to your own, but they will mirror the desperation and powerlessness that all family caregivers feel.

The point of all this is not to merely welcome you to an ever-growing club, so that you can take comfort in membership, but to add to your caregiver knowledge.

I will tell you what I learned from each episode so you can fast forward to a solution instead of floundering around in trial and error experiments of your own. Some of the lessons are so important, I have listed the critical points at the end of the story. Other memories, I feel, stand on their own without the need of a footnote.

Caregiver survival? How *do* you stay alive while watching a loved one slowly decline? Here's the short list:

---

1. Remember that it's a marathon, not a sprint.

2. Train like an athlete.

3. Breathe, deeply, slowly, and often.

4. Nourish your spirit.

5. Keep talking, working together to problem-solve.

If you understand these five rules and are nodding your head in agreement now, then reading my stories should reinforce the success of your caregiving experience. If your caregiving life, however, is itself on life-support, then picking up this book can give you hope and your own floatation device. By the time you reach the last page you should have a new attitude, a goal and a plan.

Chapter Three

PUT YOURSELF ON THE LIST

I became a caregiver in my fifties. I went from a lifetime of working 40 hours a week to a 24/7 schedule that rotated around my husband's struggle with cancer. We had been married over twenty years and all we had was each other.

Rich and I were never very social. We both worked demanding jobs and loved the time we spent together. All his people were gone, including a 33-year-old son who passed away about the time Richard started chemotherapy. I had only one functioning adult relative, my sister. The rest of my family members were very old, very young or in rehab. They all lived in other states including my sister who had her own busy career and family. Rich and I chose to have no children. We were too busy having fun—playing tennis, hiking and planning trips to Hawaii.

When Rich was first diagnosed with cancer, in addition to my Social Services career, I was active in two investment clubs—the president of one and the treasurer of another. In my spare time I was an active member of a women's service organization that raised and donated cash (in the six figure range) to a dozen local charities. I gardened. I read for pleasure. I wrote poetry. What had happened to my life?

Although devoted and attentive to my husband's growing needs, as the years dragged by, I felt I was dying inside, almost at a faster rate than he was. I was disappearing. And I didn't know how to get myself back. I tried medication for anxiety and depression (I'll talk more about that adventure later). What I eventually realized was that I couldn't remember the last time I did something for myself. Something I wanted to do, just for fun. In fact, I couldn't recall fun.

I started looking for help. I don't remember where I saw it, but it was a life-changing moment when I was shown a film about caregiving. I remember I was sitting down in a metal folding chair. The film was black and white and crackly with age.

The film opens with a couple, a little older than Rich and I were then. They are part of a joyous family get-together. All is well. In the next scene, the husband and wife are alone at home and he seems to be having some memory and behavioral issues. She is patient and kind. In the next scene he is more unruly and she is weary. She is talking on the phone, declining an invitation.

The scenes roll on, one-by-one, until she is staggering around crying at home while he throws things and falls down. The last scene is at the cemetery. It's raining. Dirt is being shoveled onto the casket in the ground. The camera turns toward the few huddled mourners. When I see who they are, I gasp. The old man is standing between two young people. The young man is holding the umbrella. The young woman says tearfully, "If Mom had only said something, we could have helped."

For a few days I pondered the message of the film. Once I got over the shock, I accepted my fate. I *was* dying, but I felt so miserable, so worthless, death seemed like a comfort. I just had to last long enough to take care of Richard. How often had I seen that happen? Two old people, one dies and the other doesn't last much longer. So, my first goal was to outlive him.

Boldly, I penciled myself in on the calendar for four hours on the following Wednesday. I didn't know what I was going to do, but I had something to look forward to, something to plan for *me*. Daydream fodder. I saw myself holding a coffee cup in my hand, giggling with a girlfriend. She's showing me pictures of her cat. I'm laughing.

Unfortunately, I didn't feel I had any friends. Richard was my best friend. I didn't have a girlfriend to giggle with on the phone. I wasn't part of a bridge club. We didn't belong to the Elks. People I knew from investing and fundraising were busy people. I couldn't imagine asking them for help in prolonging my life. And I was afraid I would just cry if I tried to ask. So, I switched to visualizing that I was getting a pedicure while I scoured my memory bank for people I've worked with—someone with an unusual last name (easily found in a Google® search) who would jump at the chance to have a cup of coffee and chat. Anybody!

---

1. If you intend to survive caregiving, you need to put yourself on your "To Do List" right up there with doctor appointments and trips to the grocery.

2. If you had four hours next Wednesday to devote to yourself, how would you fill it?

Chapter Four

WHEN NOTHING SOUNDS GOOD ENOUGH TO EAT

It's a funny thing about medication for nausea; once your stomach goes into spasm, it's already too late for the medication to be effective. There's the pill you put under your husband's tongue and the drops you squirt inside his cheek, but even if you stop the blasts from the belly, forget about him eating. And really, isn't that all you want; for him to eat something before he starts weighing less than you do?

No one tells you; not the oncologist, not the chemo-nurse, not the guy in the white coat at the drug store. No one tells you that you need to take the medication for nausea *before* you eat. It's a nau-sea-*prevention* pill. What a clever idea. Something I learned from another caregiver who routinely gave his wife her nausea medication an hour before each meal. And she *ate!*

In the first three years of illness, even with six months of chemo, Richard never complained of nausea. He seldom vomited, but he almost never ate. Nothing sounded, smelled or looked edible. He never wanted any of his nausea pills. What for? He didn't feel like throwing up, he just wasn't hungry.

I was never much of a cook but I did have a short list of things I enjoyed fixing. I made a superb spaghetti sauce from scratch with bell peppers and onions fresh from local farmer's markets. When available I added all the extra vegetables—celery, zucchini, and mushrooms—I could fit into the skillet. And there was always garlic. We loved garlic.

What really set off the sauce, however, was the handful of fresh chopped herbs from our patio. I had pots of basil, rosemary, and several flavors of oregano. After adding them, I cooked down the sauce with a little wine then added cayenne pepper at the end for extra zest. It had to cook for at least a half hour and was even better the second day. "Primavera" sauce is what Rich and I called it and we would look forward to devouring it when we had time for all that chopping and simmering.

We would prepare it together in the kitchen after a hard day at work. As the garlic-onion-herb smell filled the house we sipped wine and chatted.

In the one year that Rich was retired before he became ill he would have the kitchen ready for me when I got home. Few things can match the comfort of coming home to warm food smells and your loved one in the kitchen singing along to his favorite song.

Strong flavors were the first to go when Rich began showing signs of illness. Even before his diagnosis, the herbs and then the garlic became "too strong." The smell from first chopping the basil to simmering the completed sauce—what use to be almost as delicious as eating it—became overpowering for him. It was a very confusing time for me. I hadn't done anything differently yet everything good was suddenly wrong and I couldn't make it right.

By the time Rich's lymphoma was discovered his clothes hung on him. We were unsuccessfully trying to find food that he could eat without distress. Then he started chemotherapy and normal mealtime became a thing of the past for us.

I, at first, fixed a meal for myself and Rich had applesauce or pudding with me, but the appearance and smell of my food prevented him from eating. We concentrated on his nutrition with liquid food supplements. He kept a supply of candy bars and cookies by his chair in the living room so he could nibble whenever he was able. Consuming calories was the prime objective.

As I became busier with caregiver chores, I forgot about my own meal preparation. If I had ever actually thought about my need to eat, which I don't remember ever doing, I would have given it a very low priority. I had no fear of starving to death. I had always eaten healthy. My annual check-ups were routinely a pat-on-the-back from my doctor and a complimentary order to keep doing whatever I was doing. All my vital signs and blood work were in the low range of normal.

After Rich passed-away, when I went in for a long overdue check-up, not only had I acquired some digestive issues, but I had serious osteoporosis and my cholesterol was so high, the doctor considered putting me on medication immediately.

1. *Give your loved-one the anti-nausea pill, watch a little news together, and then start rummaging around in the kitchen.*

2. *Talk about favorite foods when he's feeling good so you'll know what to have on hand.*

3. *Don't make meal time a crisis. Don't be the food-enforcer.*

4. *Accept the fact that there will be food failures.*

5. *His favorite foods will taste "bad."*

6. *You will get tired of trying to make something he likes.*

7. *When absolutely nothing tastes good, move on. It's no one's fault. If you need to establish blame, curse the disease or the treatment.*

8. *Don't neglect your own nutritional needs. You will cope better if you fix nourishing meals and snacks for yourself.*

Chapter Five

An Invisible Means of Support

Every caregiver needs a support group. You may think you don't need one, but you do. You need a release valve to funnel off the tempest in your brain before it spews too much information all over innocent bystanders.

I embarrassed myself at the grocery store check-out stand one morning. I was piling Richard's supply of mint cookies and candy bars onto the conveyor belt when the sweet little bald-headed cashier commented on the tastiness of the Almond Joys© I was purchasing.

"Oh, they're not for me," I had to clarify. "They're for my husband. He has cancer and there isn't much he can eat, but he does have a sweet tooth and he loves Almond Joys©. It's so hard to find anything that he wants to eat..."

I continued my monologue, sparing few details. I think I even covered a colorful episode of explosive diarrhea while the shell-shocked cashier stared. It was a look like I had written "HELP ME!" in bright red letters on a sticky-note and stuck it on my forehead.

I don't remember how I got back to my car. I'm sure the cashier eagerly assisted. As I regained my breath, the humiliation set in. I dropped my head on folded arms over my steering wheel. Here I was, a reserved private person, who just spilled my guts, my innermost secrets, to someone wearing a nam-etag that I had no time to read.

I thought I was handling this caregiver thing so well, when obviously I wasn't. I didn't go to that store again for a long time and I still can't look that nice cashier in the eye. He has forgotten the incident, of course, but I haven't. I never will.

I didn't actually go looking for a caregiver support group. It found me while I was following up on a cancer patient support group for Rich. He was not enthusiastic about talking to other people with cancer, but I thought it was something he should try. So did his oncologist since he had given us the referral. It pained me to see Rich isolated at home. All his friends but one had deserted him. He only left the house on short errands, which gave him an opportunity to smoke in the car. He only left his chair in front of the TV for cigarette breaks in the garage or the backyard.

Rich did go once to the cancer patient group but he didn't feel comfortable there. He blamed his poor hearing. I, likewise, gave the offshoot group for caregivers a try. It was a warm group. They all knew each other; I was the newbie. We sat on orange vinyl sofas and chairs in a little room in the depths of the hospital. The furniture circled a coffee table where a box of fluffy pop-up tissues was the centerpiece. I went a couple of times but didn't feel it was right for me. It was, perhaps, too early in our cancer journey. Rich and I expected him to recover from lymphoma. The recovery statistics were in his favor.

A couple years later, after my grocery store meltdown, I thought again about that welcoming group huddled in the tiny room at the hospital. Rich and I were cancer veterans by then. Lymphoma had been beaten but liver cancer, a cancer with no effective treatment plans, no cures, was our new constant companion. Richard was terminal, it was only a matter of time.

When I returned to the group, I recognized two of the members (both men) from my earlier visits. They were still there. All the other faces were new to me as I was to them. The facilitator, a cancer survivor herself, had us talk one by one. The individual stories, what each caregiver had experienced in the last week, took my breath away. They were brave kindred souls, overcoming roadblocks that I thought were mine alone. Even before it was my turn to speak, I felt as if I had come home.

Find yourself a support group where you can unload the horrors of your caregiver life. They will listen to every word and even ask questions. You'll know all of them by name. They have stories of their own to tell, stories that somehow always sound worse than yours.

1. Men need a support group perhaps even more than women do.

2. Men are more resistant than women to participating in a support group.

3. A man sometimes needs another man who has been there to say, "You need a support group. You don't think you do, but you do."

4. There is something incredibly endearing about a man crying.

Chapter Six

Beyond Prune Juice

onstipation haunted us. We just couldn't get a handle on it. Richard took stool softeners, laxatives. He even "assumed the position" as he liked to call it, several times a week on all fours on the bathroom rug. (If you haven't had the pleasure of giving an adult enema, it's called the knee-chest position).

He claimed to be moving his bowels every other day, but for some reason it just wasn't enough. In the first year of his liver cancer we had a constipation crisis about every three weeks. He'd be so plugged up he couldn't sit down. Twice we went to the E.R., only to get triaged into infinity. Well, who wants to dig poop out of a frail 66 year old cancer patient's butt?

"You need a better bowel program," the E.R. nurse observed. "Well, no sh--!" is all I could think.

"Where do we get one of those?"

It wasn't until Richard went on hospice that we got educated. Hospice flushed him out and built him a bowel program from the bottom up. The really sad thing is that the pills and liquid that he took daily to stay constipation-free for the last eight months of his life could have been prescribed by his oncologist, his liver specialist or his family doctor years earlier. They weren't exotic or cutting edge or even expensive.

More important, we finally learned how to recognize and monitor normal bowel activity. Rich and I had completely missed the boat on this. Well, no one told us. When he said he "went" I took his word for it. He was a grown man. I didn't think I needed details or a sneak peek. Wrong!

1. *Think pasta machine with dough squeezed through tiny holes. Now imagine "extruded" stool, skinny curling things. What does that mean? It means you're in big trouble constipation-wise because you're so full of it that there's no room for the new softer stuff that has to snake its way around the road block or die trying.*

2. *Enema-wise, assuming "the position" should include the patient lying on his left side, knees to chest. There are anatomical advantages.*

3. *Bowel regulation is a moving target. As medications, especially narcotics, increase, so should the amount of stool agents. MiraLAX® worked great for Rich for about a year. You can buy it over the counter now without a prescription. The hospice plan included lactulose syrup (liquid) and senna-s (pills).*

4. *Check out the bowl. Fat cylinder stools are good, skinny curly ones are bad. It's so simple once you know.*

Chapter Seven

CAN I CALL SOMEONE FOR YOU?

My emergency/help list was very low tech. Just a hand-written sheet of notebook paper. I protected it in clear plastic, clamped by a strong magnet against the side of a metal filing cabinet. It's in a strategic location, just off the hall, in a room we called our study, across from the bathroom, where any social worker or highly trained medical professional would be sure to find it. Well, maybe for you, the refrigerator door would be better.

I had this nagging vision of being found rocking and hugging myself, crouched in a corner. A rescue team comes through the door. They attend to Richard. Then someone takes my hand and offers to call someone for me. And I don't know what to say.

Like any good caregiver, I suppressed those fears, until we had a crisis. The unthinkable. I got sick. We had both been exposed to megadoses of new germs. Rich got his from a five-day respite stay in a nursing home. I got mine from flying to a wedding, schmoozing with people from three Western states.

Rich was recovered enough to bring me the phone. "Yes," they said, "there was a virus going around," but unfortunately, I would have to come-in to the doctor's office to get checked-out. I made the appointment with tears in my eyes. There was no way I could drive there. I was too weak to stand.

With little discussion, Rich agreed that he should not attempt to drive me. (I was sick, not crazy.) Then, within a few minutes, shuffling around in the study, he came up with his old address book, found a name, called it and got me a ride. My hero, one more time. Unlike me, he didn't think twice about asking for help.

When I got well, I set up my list, thinking it would be used by strangers. There are first names, phone numbers, followed by keywords to identify how I know them, so that anyone could call and have an introduction. "Dale needs help. She's in your poetry group?" I mean what could be more embarrassing than placing a call and getting, "Dale, who? Never heard of her."

There are four widows on the list marked with a "W". Married friends are listed with their husband's first names. Some of the men are still in good enough shape to pitch-in for emergency handy-man jobs such as when our dining room curtain rods fell out of the wall, exposing us to that "fishbowl look." There is a friend on the list who took care of her father in his last years. Another one lives near a grocery store, so she is a prime candidate for "picking up a few things." My neighbor is listed as the one "on the right.'

When someone asks if there is anything she can do, tell her you'll be calling her. Then put her on your list and start dialing.

Chapter Eight

MEET THE REPLACEMENTS

I was just looking for a few days off. Five days actually, to fly out-of-state to see my nephew get married and visit my sister. Rich was too fragile to go and I couldn't leave him alone for long. Once, in just one hour, while I was out buying groceries, he locked himself out and fell on the patio, gashing his elbow so badly that it took a month of wound care to scab over. When I'd left him for a two-day writers conference, he was sick when I got home. Yes, a friend, as promised, had come by and taken him to lunch, but didn't stick around for the next twenty-four hours to handle the restaurant food aftermath.

When hospice suggested respite care in a nursing home, it sounded like a good deal. Rich would have 24/7 attention, warm meals, a supply of on-time medications and an opportunity to socialize, something I was always trying to nudge his way.

The wedding wasn't until May, but we started the selection process months earlier. I took a nurse friend to coffee and scribbled on a Starbucks© napkin. Two lists. The five best nursing homes in our area and the five worst. Where she would go if she were incapacitated versus places that might kill you if you stayed there.

Rich and I made drop-in, unscheduled visits. It took over a month because one trip on a good day pushed the limits of his stamina. We gave them all the "whiff test" and checked for activity and happy faces. We eliminated one because the rooms didn't have TV. The other four seemed fine. When the time came, only one had an opening. That's the scary thing about nursing home respite care. You can do all the planning you want, but availability is the key. You only have "open beds" to pick from no matter where they are.

The facility promised to meet all of Rich's needs. Yes, he would have a TV with closed captioning in his room. Yes, I could bring a supply of his favorite tapioca to be kept in the small refrigerator at the nurse's station. The placement director told us to arrive early in the day so we could meet the dietician to ensure the foods that he could eat. Yes, the nice bath-aide who helped him shower twice a week at home could keep on schedule and assist him at the nursing home.

It started out badly and never got better. When we showed up on the appointed check-in morning, no one was expecting us. In hindsight Rich would have done better left at home with a series of drop-in visitors than what did happen to him, most of which I didn't hear about until after my trip.

In five days they never gave him drinking water. He never got a side table on wheels either so maybe that was the problem (no place to put the pitcher of water). When he asked for water they gave him a thimble-sized pill cup. He asked about bottled water in the vending machine and was told the machine hadn't worked in ages, contrary to the commentary on our walk-through tour.

They neither had his medications nor a sense of urgency that they should get them. They wouldn't allow pain pills brought from home, so I got to make frantic calls to hospice and the pharmacy delivery driver while I was packing my suitcase.

Rich couldn't eat the food. It was all pureed and tasted nasty. He never got to eat any of the dozen tapioca cups that I wrote his name on in fat, black ink. They were thrown out at the first nurse shift change. We never met the dietician although she was scheduled to meet with Rich about his preferences on the day I took him home.

The bathing arrangements didn't pan out. When the bath-aide showed up at the usual time, all the showers were full or spoken for. No one mentioned that you had to sign up for a shower stall. So, the only bathing Rich got was a quick soaping and a hand-held rinse in a dark corner.

Rich was alone in his room during the day so he got some sleep. At night his roommate's PTSD (post traumatic stress disorder) outbursts and oxygen machine thumping made it impossible. There was no telephone in his room. When I called him he used the phone at the nurses station where he was afraid to verbalize anything besides he was "doing fine." I could have gotten him a cell phone if I had known he would be standing out in the hall, but then what would I have done from afar to help?

"Did you have a good time at the wedding? Did you enjoy your trip?" That's all Rich wanted to know when I started hyperventilating as I heard the details of his nursing home stay. Yes, it was great to be somewhere else, having fun. And Rich did survive thanks to hospice personnel and a friend who came by to take him on "outings" which mostly involved bringing him home to relax and get stuff.

To be fair, they did come through with the in-room closed captioned TV. If there are decent nursing homes out there, Rich and I spent a lot of time looking, yet didn't experience one. But I learned what I needed to know. No matter how terminal he was, I would never give another nursing home a chance to kill him.

---

1. Plan ahead

Don't wait until you are "ready to drop" to plan respite for yourself and care for your loved one. If you do, you will come home to a disaster, which spells more work for you, hardship for your loved one, and years of guilt to look forward to. Although, it is not natural to us and may feel selfish, it is *never* too soon to plan time to get away.

---

2. Make a list of caregiver chores that need to be done on a daily basis.

Be realistic. Simplify it down to what is absolutely necessary. Yes, you may preheat his towels and cut his sandwiches into four pieces, but don't ask a temporary helper to provide those extras. Focus on what will keep him alive and comfortable while you are away recharging your battery.

*3. Review your list, picturing
someone else doing these tasks.*

Imagine your next-door neighbor popping in twice a day to give medication and whipping up a bowl of oatmeal. Visualize your brother stopping by after work a few days in a row to get him ready for bed.

Caution 1: You will have trouble with this. No one will give him care as well as you do. Close your eyes. Take a deep breath and accept that fact. You are putting in second-string rookies as your re-placement. Get over it and move on. If you are to go the distance as a caregiver you *need* time away. Your patient can handle a few days without your pampering but you will not make it to the end of the caregiving marathon, if you don't refuel along the way.

Caution 2: Be prepared for resistance from your ill loved one. He wants you and needs you every day. You are his whole world. Anticipate his objections but do not give in. Do not let him sabotage your respite plans. Your life as well as his depends on you having relief. In a perfect world, you would sit down and review your list of tasks with your loved-one.

His input would be valuable. He could tell you what he needs the most and what he could get along without until you return. You might be surprised at his choices.

Caution 3: If your loved-one is still cognitively aware, give him time to accept that you need a vacation and will be gone for a few days. Let him rant, cry, curse, shame you while you are still there so that by the time you leave he will be tired of protesting and mellowed into a more cooperative patient for your replacement. Having a pleasant experience for patient, fill-in help and you is essential if you are to make respite care a regular part of your schedule. If your loved-one rebels and makes life miserable for your replacements, future respites will be nightmares to arrange, if possible at all.

---

*4. Choose who will provide the
care while you are gone.*

If the tasks are simple and friends, neighbors and family can be coordinated to cover for you, get on the phone and make it happen. Remember all those people who said, "Let me know if I can do anything?" Now is their time. Schedule everyone in and give them all a copy of the calendar so they know when they are "on duty" and who will relieve them. Ask them to call each other (not you) if scheduling changes occur while you are gone.

If you do not have a support network or if the caregiving tasks are too difficult or too numerous, hire someone to come to your home and take your place while you are gone. The most expensive replacement will be a nurse. If you don't need nurse level care, hire an experienced caregiver. There are lots of agencies that specialize in this.

If you have time and want to lower the price, get a list of independent contracting caregivers and do your own screening, referral calling and interviewing. You can get such a list from local public social service agencies or you can advertise yourself.

Caution 1: Running your own caregiver-wanted ad is time-consuming and more risky than using a caregiver placement agency. Agencies handle insurance, bonding and payroll issues that you probably don't want to deal with. Paying benefits for employed caregivers is an evolving gray area of responsibility. Like live-in maids and nannies these hard workers deserve basic benefits but do you have the knowledge or strength to cope with this added task?

Caution 2: Just because someone is on a caregiver list doesn't mean they are well-qualified, experienced, honest or even compassionate. Remember, this person will be alone in your home for hours at a time with your fragile loved one.

---

5. *With your loved-one, meet and interview any caregiver who will be in your home.*

If an agency says they have several "on-call" people to fill-in during unexpected shortages, ask to interview *all* of them. Both you and your loved-one should feel comfortable with your temporary replacement(s).

I have two personal examples of the importance of this step.

My father lost his ability to walk in the last year of his life. I moved him to foster care where he sat in his recliner all day, too vacant to even watch TV. He had looked forward to physical therapy sessions but insurance stopped paying for them because he was not capable of improvement. Alzheimer's had destroyed his muscle memory as well as his cognitive abilities.

In an attempt to provide the social interaction that he seemed to enjoy I hired a soft-spoken man, a career caregiver with excellent references. He already had two long-term commitments with families who sang his praises, yet he was still willing to drop by and see Dad a couple times a week for a reasonable hourly rate.

On their first visit, Dad's new friend took him out for coffee, tenderly packing him up in his car. Dad had not been outside or done anything fun in so long, I was thrilled and so proud of my success as a good daughter.

Dad, however, did not share my delight. He wanted to know, in his broken cognitive babble, who was this guy and why was he was hanging around? We tried a couple more meetings until Dad spit out flatly with uncharacteristic expletives that he didn't like the guy. Too bad I hadn't included Dad in the interview.

I made a different mistake with my mother. After Mom broke her hip I hired a caregiver to help her several times a week with errands and simple household chores. Mom was sharp although plagued by numerous physical limitations. I valued her opinion. During the interview process the caregiver mentioned that her back-up, if she should be unable to make a scheduled shift, was her niece.

I asked probing questions about the niece's qualifications but I did not meet her in person. After Mom met her for the first time I asked Mom what she thought. Mom thought she was "very young" but "trainable" and that she would be fine.

The young woman had been described to me as qualified because she had provided similar assistance to her grandparents for several years. In fact, as the story was told to me, if it weren't for the help of the niece living with and helping the elderly couple they would not be able to remain in their home.

When I did meet the young woman it was in the E.R. She had the appearance and the judgment of a twelve-year-old. She had taken my mother to the grocery store in a monster truck and let her fall out of the cab onto her face in the parking lot. Mom broke not only her nose but also both wrists.

---

6. *Avoid nursing homes for short-term respite care.*

Staff turnover in nursing homes is high and adequate care is unpredictable, which spells tremendous risk for a short-term stay. If you must move your loved-one to a temporary, unfamiliar location for adequate care while you are gone, check out adult foster care in your area. Not available in all states and usually only for a month or longer stay, foster care is far superior and less costly than a nursing home facility.

Chapter Nine

LET IT OUT WITH A SIGH

I didn't think I would like yoga. I was more of a tennis, hiking, dancing kind of gal. But "Caregiver Yoga," a series of introductory restorative sessions was free and I needed *me time* in my calendar. So, I went and it changed my life. It helped, of course, that we were all caregivers. I looked around at my peers—all women past our prime—and sighed. These were my people, beasts of burden with broken spirits, quietly resting, waiting.

Restorative yoga poses require numerous props and lots of lying around doing nothing. My back and shoulders loved being sprawled over folded blankets. My heels felt great up against a wall. My arms melted into the cushiony folds as I stretched myself out and played dead.

And the breathing! It was magnificent. I realized how shallow I had been breathing.

My breath was tension-locked inside me. I had forgotten how to exhale.

I finished the caregiver sessions, loving every single one. Yoga practice pulled emotion from the depths of my body. Most final resting poses found me with tears running into my ears, trying hard to stifle a guttural sob. My instructor encouraged me to not stifle, to give in and let the feeling happen. "It's very common," she said. "Grief hidden so deep, we don't even know it's there."

And it was a wonderful feeling—not like real crying. Yes, there were tears and a wail perhaps but the sensation was pleasant, more like gulping cool water after a long run on a hot day.

Yoga's convenience worked for me. I didn't have to arrange for a partner, reserve a court or "Google" a route map. I didn't have to prepare for a yoga class or compete when I got there. I didn't have to interact with anyone. I didn't even have to talk. I could count on not being interrupted for sixty to ninety minutes. I let my mind take a mini-vacation while my body reminded me how good it could feel to be alive.

Yoga still works for me. My yoga mat has a permanent place on my floor. My daily practice may be long or short but it still quiets my mind and allows my body to fondly remember that it was once young.

—⟶⟨⟩⟵—

1. *Yoga instruction ranges from gentle and therapeutic to hot, sweaty and for extreme-athletes only.*

2. *Never go to a yoga class without talking to the instructor first.*

3. *The teacher as well as the type of yoga must be right for you.**

4. *If you get bored with the basic poses, check out partner yoga (practicing with someone who matches your size and capabilities.)*

—⟶⟨⟩⟵—

*I attempted to endure a humiliating yoga class in which the instructor was all about impressing us with her supple expertise. She demeaned me into hurting myself but I left while I could still walk.

Chapter Ten

JUST *BE* WITH ME

In five years of enduring cancer, Richard never relied on medication for depression or anxiety. When he felt panic, he would call me to hold his hand.

The first time he called me from the kitchen to the bedroom, I expected the worst. "Can you be with me for awhile?" he said calmly as he lay in bed. "Hold my hand." There was no apparent crisis. Relieved, I took his right hand with mine and placed my left over them both. He closed his eyes and looked restful against his pillow. "You're going to get tired bending over like that," he said after a couple of deep breaths. I brought in a chair from another room and found it equally uncomfortable. The bed was too high. The chair was too low; my arm too tense. But I didn't need to be there long. His breathing deepened and he fell asleep.

You listen to a lot of stories when your marriage spans decades. You hear about the deep hidden places that shape who you are and how you got to this point in time.

I'd heard Rich's ironworker stories a thousand times, and a few times he shared the ones about the power of touch in a crisis. The first incident happened before I knew him, in a machine shop with a man dangling from a platform.

"Go up there and talk to him," the foreman barked at Rich (a twenty-year-old gofer at the time), "so he don't go in ta shock." Rich got up on a ladder on another platform and leaned out to the suspended man.

"He was really scared," Rich said. "You could see it in his face."

As Rich talked, I saw the man's face as if I had been there. It was a face, white with fear. Eyes glowing, wide with terror. Breath pounding out rapid beats.

"But I took his hand and I told him 'everything's going to be all right' and you could see he felt better."

As Rich continued, I saw the man change. His breath lengthening, eyes were closing, face softening, a hint of color.

"I stayed with him until the ambulance came."

We were married when the second work incident happened late in Rich's ironworker career. An apprentice tried to tame a high-pressure hose that coiled up like a snake and slammed him against a concrete wall. The young man sat motionless at the bottom of the wall where he had dropped into a sitting position. Rich put down his tools and went over to him, took his hands and talked softly to him. "His face was white and he was staring, but after awhile he came around. I could feel it in his hands."

"Don't go anywhere," Rich said to me… "Just *be* with me."

I wanted to do more, to stroke his hand, to squeeze it, but I was missing the point. He opened one eye.

"Just *be* with me." His voice was soft but stern. He only had to tell me once. I smile every time I think of it, his telling me in words what he needed when I could not feel it. "Hold my hand, but don't rub it."

Chapter Eleven

MEDICATING THE CAREGIVER

Richard didn't feel the need for depression medication. I wasn't so lucky. Of course, I waited until I couldn't function. All I did was cry. But unlike Rich who floated through the 60's, I was a drug virgin. When, between sobs, I got prescription help for depression, anxiety and muscle tension, I torpedoed myself into uncharted waters.

The fast talking guy wearing the Vehicle Emissions Inspection badge kept asking me to set the hand brake. Hand. Brake. My brain waited unsuccessfully for an image. I sat in my bucket seat staring at the radio. I knew I should be looking for something and I was taking too long but I didn't care that I couldn't find it. It was so unlike me. No panic. No sweat. Hmmm. Well, well.

He held the door of my Honda™ open with his left hand and pointed over my lap with his right.

I scanned the cup holder. Hmmm. Well, well. An arm whizzed past my T-shirt and swooped over my right hand. "Here, ma'am. It's right here." "Oh," was my dreamy response. "I guess. I don't. Use it. Much." A black rod at my right elbow.

I watched my thumb press the silver button on the end and pull up. Then I had to "step out and wait behind the glass." I made it to the enclosed waiting area. No seats, just a walkway with a chest-high shelf mounted under windows where I leaned, led by my purse.

The overhead sign advised me to not write my check until my vehicle had passed inspection. This was getting hard; too much thinking. "Hmm," I thought. "I better get started." I didn't want the cashier to have to help me like the guy fiddling with my car.

Purse. Checkbook. Pen. Cap covering pen. The date flowed onto the proper line. I knew not to put in a dollar amount. I didn't know what it was yet. At the cash register I think my hand shook a little while I filled in the two empty lines on my check, but the person behind the counter (I think it was a woman) didn't hurry me.

The next thing I remember was being in my car, waiting to turn into traffic. The light changed to green and I didn't know what to do. "Oh my

God," I thought. "I don't know what I'm doing." I should have been panicked, but panic seemed so far away. I was floating in a bubble, just trying to get home.

I merged right, into traffic. I only had to make a couple turns. There was a left at the next light and then I could just go straight for a long time. I thought I would recognize my street when I got close. Why was I doing this today? I had plenty of time to have my car checked for emissions. My plate didn't expire until October. But an hour earlier, thanks to modern pharmacology, the fog inside my head lifted. The sun was shining and I jumped at the chance to drive around and queue up in it's warmth.

Once home, I reasoned that some fresh-air activity would clear my head. As I staggered through the garage I picked up my gardening bucket and sailed out to the backyard to do a little weeding.

I do remember falling face-first into the ground cover. Apparently, getting down to the weeds was more than my motor skills could manage. I spent the rest of the afternoon sprawled out in the bedroom watching the ceiling, listening to my breathing. I vaguely remembered seeing Rich when I climbed into the kitchen from the patio but I didn't know where he was and I didn't care.

1. *Don't believe doctors when they say it takes two weeks for mood changing medication to take effect. I cut small starter dosages in half and went "blotto" in less than three days.*

2. *Chemically treating caregiver depression and anxiety is serious business. Who needs one more problem to deal with?*

3. *Yoga and my support group never looked so good.*

Chapter Twelve

OXYGEN FOR WHAT AILS YOU

"Where did the cat go?" Rich asked. I looked away from the TV to where he was staring. We had never shared our home with a cat.

"What cat?"

"The one that was walking around the pictures." He pointed to the framed photographs lined up on the stone ledge in front of the fireplace. "It was stepping around all those pictures. But I don't see it now."

"You saw a cat there." He didn't seem to be concerned that he was hallucinating, but I was. I tried to sound casual. "So, what did it look like?" Without hesitation he described an agile tabby right down to the white paws.

It wasn't until the next morning that he agreed he couldn't have seen a cat. Together we pondered the illusion, hoping there would be no more. But in the days that followed there were other incidents. He conversed with people I didn't see. He questioned me about imaginary events I was supposed to have taken part in.

Was this the confusion, I wondered, that rode along with end stage liver disease? He seemed too normal to be working up to a bell-ringing psychotic meltdown. Most of the time he was fine.

When Rich's hospice nurse came on Monday, we had plenty to tell her. She was such a good listener with such great probing questions. After poking and measuring, she offered a solution. "Richard, have you ever used oxygen?" Ah, if the nurse had only known. Rich dreamed of sucking up oxygen. "Just quit smoking" I would scoff unsympathetically whenever he brought it up.

She wanted Rich to try it at night. She suspected his brain was gasping for oxygen, while his cancer-struggling body claimed every breath for basic functions, like keeping him alive. "I'll order it," she said. Rich beamed. He could hardly wait for her to leave so he could shuffle out to the garage for a celebratory cigarette.

When the delivery truck pulled up out front, I had no idea the driver was going to empty half of the truck's contents into my living room. Three trips; two with a hand truck. First he brought in the back-up tank of pure oxygen (four-feet tall mounted on a three-foot square metal frame) to be used if the power ever went out. Then came the bags of plastic tubing and brightly colored hardware that I would string together into 50 feet stretching from the oxygen source to Rich's nose.

Then a bulky two-foot square cabinet, like a safe on wheels rolled across the entryway linoleum and came to an abrupt stop when it hit the carpet. The oxygen concentrator (ready to make my life miserable) waited for a proper introduction.

The driver handed me a 39 page manual and spewed off instructions. He pointed to where water needed to be added. The filter needed to be cleaned and replaced. There was a schedule for maintaining the plastic tubing. "Oh great," I mumbled under my breath, "more stuff for me to worry about." The driver slapped a "NO SMOKING" sticker on the front door on his way out.

An oxygen concentrator, unlike a passive tank of compressed gas, pulls oxygen out of the air around it. It's a working piece of equipment. It sounds four even beeps, like a truck backing up, every time it's turned on, and then settles into a mechanical drone. A monotonous compressor noise interrupted with a two-step thump followed by a barely audible echoed chime.

Even with his good ear down on the pillow, Rich couldn't sleep with the concentrator near the bedroom. We wanted to stuff the thing in a closet or banish it to the garage, but evidently we were not the first to think of this because both locations were specifically forbidden in the instruction manual. The concentrator had to be in an open room, no less than three feet from anything.

We tried the kitchen but too much echoing off the tile. The living room was a little better as it had lots of soft surfaces to absorb noises. I spent the first night moving the little beast all over the room in search of a good spot but the cord was too short, and using extensions was strictly forbidden. I eyed the cozy corner where the monument-like emergency tank sat, chained to its metal platform. But I didn't want to wrestle with it, especially in my nightgown.

Even with my bedroom door closed, I listened for the thump and strained to hear the chime. *Vroom, thump, thump, pause, ting.*

Thankfully, Rich was able to finally sleep and he never saw another imaginary cat. On the down side, he became increasingly dependent on oxygen and eventually he couldn't breathe for long without it.

Nosebleeds became a problem in spite of the concentrator's humidifier system. Saline nasal spray (like OCEAN®) worked well. K-Y Jelly® helped with irritations from the plastic nosepieces. Rich enjoyed his coveted oxygen supply and thankfully, continuous use left little time for smoke breaks in the garage. We both got what we wanted, after all.

Chapter Thirteen

NOT ON MY TOWEL!

"He doesn't talk to me." The tiny lady squirmed in her chair and pulled her polyester print dress tightly down over her knees. Her hands crossed to her elbows as she hugged herself and continued her story. She didn't drive and she was stuck in a tiny apartment with her dying husband who treated her like a maid from a third world country. "He comes out of the bedroom, walks outside to smoke. Doesn't say nothin' to me, like I'm not even there." Several of the other caregivers in the room nodded.

"I know it's hard." The matronly facilitator stepped away from her flip chart and focused on the woman. "My husband completely ignores me too." I thought she might burst into tears. I could not believe what I was hearing. And all that nodding of approval and understanding. Could she be condoning bad behavior?

So uncool for a facilitator, I thought. She was supposed to be in-charge. The rest of us came for support and direction and to cry during our allotted turn. I was not prepared to listen to how I should grin and bear verbal brutality.

"Why do women put up with this?" I wondered. A guy is dying of cancer and the woman who is busting her tail keeping him alive and comfortable gets treated like a fly-infested plough horse? What is wrong with this picture? Caregivers need reciprocal hugs.

I refused to believe that Rich was a saint (I knew better) but these caregivers seemed to be suffering beyond the call of duty. I didn't understand their acceptance, yet I could relate to how it happens.

Rich and I had talked at the beginning of his illness about my limitations. "I'm not a nurse and I'm not a farm girl," I'd said. I had worked in offices all my life. So, I was just a 5' 5", white-collar worker, with puny arms and a stiff "computer" neck. Yet, he resisted my early attempts to make my job easier.

I suggested upgrading our glass-enclosed tub/shower but I had to lie to get his approval, right down to the grab bar. I said "I" needed it. He scoffed at having "stand-by" help from a bath-aide when he took a shower until he fell backwards and landed on the shower seat.

He tried to shame me by saying that the bath-aides probably wondered why someone young and strong like me needed help.

He was dying. I wanted to love him, not argue. I passively skirted confrontation while I picked up after him and bit my lip as his litter filled our home, turning it into a hospital suite. I felt like I was "flopping" at a friend's house because I had somehow gotten squeezed out. I even struggled for a place to hang my bath towel.

Unlike my toothbrush and lotions, which had been stowed away long ago with all my other personal stuff, the towel needed a place to dry out. Rich had his two favorite towels (none of the others were soft enough). So, it was obvious which one was mine; the one that I kept moving around to be out of his way.

The day came when I walked into the bathroom and found my towel violated. A soppy washcloth had been flung into the middle of it. I stared at the soaked washcloth oozing into my towel on the towel bar and my negotiation skills and positive attitude abandoned me.

I steadied myself with a deep breath and stomped out to the living room. "How dare you," I growled. "You may be sick, but you're not *that* sick. I live here too…" Rich stopped me with an apology before I could properly vent.

"I knew when I did it, I shouldn't have. It won't happen again." I wanted to rant more but once more he cut me off. "I said, I won't do it again." And he never did.

---

1. *I had to stand up for myself. I had to identify unacceptable behavior and demand respect.*

2. *If you don't like being treated like a nameless domestic for hire, then start acting like the strong organized crisis manager that you are.*

Chapter Fourteen

Hospices By the Dozen

"I t's probably a good time for you to get acquainted with the hospice people," Rich's oncologist said. The chubby-cheeked doctor, fifty pounds over-weight, such a rude appearance I always thought for a physician specializing in scrawny cancer patients, grinned and said "they" would be calling just to "meet us." And so, without a single comment from Rich or me, "hospice" was unleashed on us. As often happens when decisions are made without user input, we were awarded not the "A" but the "F" Hospice Team.

The telephone started ringing. People we didn't know introduced themselves quickly and auto-matically, offering vague things I did not understand. At the end of the monologue there was always a persistent request to "stop by."

"Who are all these people?" Rich asked.

"I don't know."

The "F" Team hospice nurse spent the first part of her visit scolding us about Rich's driving.

"Oh, if he ever gets stopped and the police find out he's on pain medication, you'll lose your house and everything you've ever owned!" She shuddered and threw her paperwork on our kitchen table, carefully cupping her hand so she didn't chip an acrylic nail. Her perfect manicure dashed any hope we might have that she would be providing any hands-on care.

When she was done chastising us and completely alienating us from ever wanting to speak to her again, she started bragging about her grand-daughter. There were pictures and stories about her "cuteness."

"I'm not going to stop driving," Rich said when we closed the door behind her.

"I know."

How any nurse, let alone a hospice nurse, could know so little about narcotics and long-term pain management was beyond our comprehension.

True, Rich's dosage of oxycontin would have killed an elephant, but he had worked up to that level through three years of pain escalation. Without pain medication he couldn't function. He wasn't out joy-riding, tearing up the town. He smoked in his car as he drove around the neighborhood. The oncologist (old chubby cheeks) had told him he was fine to drive as long as he stayed in our zip code and avoided the freeway.

Months earlier Rich had confided in me that as long he could still drive, he was "all right," probably because he was getting too weak to stand outside or in the garage. He had never smoked in the house.

The "F" Team social worker looked like she was eighteen and acted like a twelve-year-old fresh from her first customer service workshop. She had a scripted answer, delivered with phony rote inflection in response to my questions. I stopped asking. She had no experience in the real world and absolutely didn't give a flying fig.

The last straw fell when I tried to get help from her. I understood that as a hospice patient Rich was entitled to a "bath-aide" at least once a week. He had already fallen backwards into the shower and he was more than I could handle by myself. When the social worker finally took my call, her automated response brought me to tears.

"I know" (pause). "It's hard."

After listening to several repetitions of these four cold syllables, I hung up the phone and sobbed.

My support group, once again, came to the rescue. The facilitator of the group, good old Katy knew the hospice unit manager. Within 24 hours we went from Team F to Team A+. Both the nurse and the social worker were wonderful. All the good things people say about hospice are actually true.

1. You have choices.

If you search online for hospice services in your city, thousands of results will likely appear. Keep that in mind when your doctor starts talking about hospice care as if it were a single off-the-shelf service. You don't have to just blink and wait for the crowd to show up at your front door. Your doctor will link you with the hospice plan that is affiliated with his practice and his hospital privileges. That's a referral made out of convenience and business protocol, not an indication of quality or suitability for what you need. Shop hospice providers like you would when getting estimates for carpeting if you have to. Let them fight over your business because realistically that's what you are to them.

2. Hospice services are specifically defined by law and universal.

Medicare, Medicaid and insurance providers supply all of the same defined benefits. There is no such thing as a less comprehensive or abbreviated plan. They may offer additional benefits such as a harpist to play at your loved one's bedside, but they can't skimp on the basic comfort care package.

The only difference between one provider and another is the way they deliver the services. For example, a wheelchair or walker should be size appropriate for the patient. If your hospice provider drops off a wheelchair without measuring the patient or offering options for a seat cushion, the chair likely will not be comfortable enough to be used. How about pain management? You want hospice services that deliver morphine in the middle of the night when your loved one needs it, not an organization that has nothing but voicemail on the weekends.

Your hospice team should be a band of angels to you. They should anticipate your needs before you even think to ask. If your team is not like that sign up with another company.

---

3. Don't wait.
Once treatments and other curative
measures are exhausted and comfort
becomes the sole objective, there is no
point in trying to coordinate care and
available resources on your own.

Hospice comforts both patient and caregiver in ways you can't imagine. Let them do it sooner rather than later.

---

4. *There is no time limit to hospice.*

Rich received hospice care for almost nine months.

---

5. *A patient can graduate from hospice by getting better. If he gets worse, he can always receive hospice care again.*

Chapter Fifteen

SPLITTING THE SHEETS

I didn't sleep much in 2003, the year of Rich's first cancer (lymphoma) but it didn't seem important. I was on a mission to avoid what I feared was the inevitable—waking up to find him dead beside me. Chemotherapy was slowly sucking the life out of him. He was a walking corpse during the day, but at night he slept on his back, motionless, so it was hard to tell if he was alive or not. I spent my nights routinely testing for movement, listening for breath. "Yep, still breathing," I'd tell myself when he responded to my light touch under the covers.

The second cancer (primary liver cancer) brought with it high doses of pain medication and nightmares. Rich slept but his body never rested. His legs would spasm, propelling at least one of his size 14 feet in my direction. He cried out in sharp, angry threats. He thrust his left arm straight up and wrote in the air with his left hand, which is strange because he was right-handed.

My dozing would be broken with a scream. He whimpered and thrashed, unable to find his way out of his dream. It took rough shaking to wake him, and then I held him, kissing his forehead, as he sobbed. In the mornings he seemed fine but I was exhausted.

By 2006, sleep deprivation was making me cranky. The nightmares had subsided, but the flying arms and legs had not. They appeared nightly with guttural dialogue. "I can't do this anymore," I told Rich. "I've got to get some sleep." He suggested we buy a single bed for me and set it up in one of the other bedrooms.

"Oh, no," I protested. "We don't need to go to all that trouble." Rich was always thinking long term, while I was thinking "what am I going to do with an extra bed when he's gone?" We went shopping for a temporary solution and came home with two foam rubber pads. They were cushions to be used under sleeping bags but I put them one on top of the other so that I had eight inches of mattress. I threw them on the floor in the bedroom across the hall and curled up with my favorite pillow between folded sheets.

I did sleep better that night, but we both missed the pillow talk. I'm not talking about sex. Cancer had taken that from us a long time ago. I'm talking about that conversation that flows easily once the lights are out and you're settling down with your #1 fan. The everyday things in whispered tones to someone who knows your history because he's lived it with you.

The first night Rich and I shouted out our pillow talk across the hall but it was awkward especially since Rich was practically deaf. I tried going to bed with him and then getting up and moving across the hall, but then I couldn't fall asleep.

I bought a real single mattress and frame in 2007. I didn't mind getting up and down from the floor to sleep on the foam pads, but manipulating them to change the sheets took more energy than I felt I could ration.

The creation of my caregiver bed was an emotional milestone, the acceptance of change in our relationship, the end of our lives as lovers. Rich would never again be that passionate man I married. He was my dear sick friend, my little boy… my baby. I was his caregiver.

By 2008 Rich was in bed most of the time, surrounded by paraphernalia to keep him comfortable. So, at some point I would have had to find my own bed. I probably should have let him sleep alone sooner than I did, but it was a hard thing to give up. Losing a life companion involves so many losses, all of which look better with a good night's sleep.

Chapter Sixteen

ONE WIDOW–TWO LISTS

R ich wanted to know what things were on my list. Not his usual way of requesting store supplies. "You need more mint cookies?" I asked. He never could say the "d" word so he cleared his throat and rearranged the junk mail in front of him on the kitchen table as I waited. "No, your list… things you'll need… later."

It took me a moment. I never used the "d" word either. I searched for a better way to say it but couldn't get past the obvious. "You mean when I'm a widow?"

I actually did have a widow's list, a fanciful list of things to look forward to that kept me going when things got rough. Once I had made the decision that there was life for me after caregiving, I needed to picture myself actually doing things in that single life.

It took many daydreams to come up with something that would give me pleasure, something I had always wanted to do. I needed goals. It was a pivotal moment when I thought of myself dancing as if I didn't have a care in the world. My mental widow's list started with the entry "learn to tango" with sub-tasks "price lessons at Arthur Murray" and "shop for black dress with above-the-knee slit."

I didn't think this was the list Rich was referring to. He might have misunderstood this survival exercise. I had never written my list down.

Rich meant a practical, more immediate list. He and the hospice social worker had discussed ways he could still be my hero. Were there things he could do to help me now so I wouldn't have to do them alone later?

He stared like a little boy hoping against hope, embarrassed by the absurdity of his own question. I wanted to kiss him.

I saw us on the carousel. Rich is standing, not sitting, but standing all of his six feet tall. The mechanical hurdy-gurdy beat fades from my ears into a soft pulse as Rich gallantly extends his hand to me, beckoning me to get off my lacquered pony, to forget about jousting for him.

I cannot disappoint him. "Well yes, I do have a list."

"You do?" Rich brightened and sat back in his chair.

I took an empty envelope from the stack of opened mail and reached for a pen. "The furnace. It's noisy. I've always hated it and I can't change the filters by myself."

"I know. Your arms are too short. Let's get you a new furnace… and air-conditioning," He beamed. "What else?"

Within a few minutes we had a list and Rich was all over it. He couldn't wait to tackle the first project, replacing our old dangerously-worn, six-foot wooden ladder. He was eager to check out aluminum ones that would be easy for me to set up under our magnolia tree and lift up to a storage hook in the garage. He drove to Home Depot® by himself to evaluate them.

It was June 10, 2008. I know the date because he got a speeding ticket (the kind they mail to your house with the picture of you sitting behind the wheel) for going 32 MPH in a 20 MPH School Zone, a well-known speed trap that he had warned me about on a regular basis.

Several days later, we went to Home Depot® so I could make the final selection. He had me fold them and open them up. He pointed out the importance of keeping the sidebars level and locked. And, of course, I should never use one in a storm or lean it against electrical wires.

Years earlier I would have indignantly reminded him that I am not an idiot. Instead I listened
intently, chose one with his approval (it had a
drop-down shelf suitable for holding a can of
paint) then I loaded it on a platform cart for its
ride to the check stand.

Together we worked through the list. We gave
away a stack of firewood from the backyard that
had been moved twice but seldom used in twenty
years. We put casters on my butcher block in
the kitchen. We had two overgrown sweet gums
removed from the parking strip so I wouldn't have
to rake leaves or worry about a broken sidewalk.
The final item on the list, the heating and air
conditioning unit which was installed the end of
August, is a story all its own.

Our written widow's list was a gift we gave to
each other. The gift of enjoying one more summer
together with "things to do" that didn't involve
doctors, pills or dying. I could have handled all
those projects on my own, probably more quickly
and more efficiently. But thanks to my rescuing
knight, I didn't have to.

1. Let your loved one feel useful.

2. Make memories together.

Chapter Seventeen

Last Call

The soft-spoken hospice social worker sitting in my living room said I had a decision to make. The nurse standing next to her waited for a reply. Too many things were coming all at once in the heat of August 2008. A three-man air conditioning crew stomped past us, banging their equipment against the front screen door on the way to the basement as the nurse and the social worker waited for me to speak. I listened to the loud male voices, lively testosterone-laced banter, echoing off the wooden stairs.

Then it hit me… I had to give him up.

Rich and I had reached the point where I could not take care of him anymore. He needed 24/7 care that I alone could not provide. I needed to either hire around-the-clock in-home care or move him to a place where he could get it. Their urgency stunned me.

Yes, Rich had a commode by his bed which we were having trouble navigating together. A wheelchair had been ordered so he could get to the living room. Subtle changes I thought. The nurse and the social worker, however, knew worse things were coming, soon. This was the beginning of the end. The last song before the carousel stopped. The moment I had dreaded since 2003 when our family doctor, seated on a white metal stool, calmly faced Richard and said, "you have cancer."

I had to shop for qualified, trustworthy people to bring into our home or find a safe, fully-equipped place where Richard would comfortably die. That's what they were telling me. We were just days away from a three-day weekend. Monday would be Labor Day. I didn't have much time.

I could hear the men in the basement tearing out the old furnace as I envisioned a parade of strangers coming in shifts every eight hours while I hovered watching them. What if someone called in sick and no one showed up? What if they ransacked my purse while I nodded off in a chair? What if I didn't like what they did to Rich?

How long would I be living in an ICU? Rich could go on for months. He'd already been on hospice since January 1st. Certainly he wanted to pass away at home in his own bed. But I was tired and afraid. I would not be sleeping while he struggled through end stage liver disease. I would be a hand-wringing spectator. I couldn't bear to think of it, let alone watch it unfold over days or weeks. I wouldn't survive it. And after all, I had made that decision in my second year of caregiving, that yes, I wanted to live. I wanted to survive.

Since nursing homes were out (*see Chapter Eight*) my only choice was adult foster care. There actually was a foster care home on my street. I had stopped in during one of my walks to ask about respite care. A pleasant middle-aged Russian woman took care of five patients there. I liked her. It was a family business as all foster care homes are, with her family living in the other half of the house.

The hospice duo steered me to Richard's bedroom to update him on my decision. The nurse took center stage. She got only a few words out when the room shook to the ring of sledgehammer on metal. The old furnace was directly under Rich's bed. She paused, then started again with the same interruption. "Can you go tell them to give us ten minutes?"

I obeyed, clomping down the stairs to break up the work party, telling them to take a break. We were having an important conversation and needed to hear what the hospice nurse had to say. Three young men, late twenties early thirties stared blankly at me. I wondered if they had ever heard of hospice, let alone know what it meant.

The rest of the morning was a blur. The afternoon found me calling foster care homes, working down a fifteen-page county list downloaded from the internet. Rich wanted something that made my search very difficult—a room with a private (not shared) bath—an unheard of accommodation for a bed-ridden man. I was laughed at and ridiculed when I asked, but guilt kept me going. Rich wanted a private bathroom so that he could put his oxygen machine in it and close the door. He dreaded the concentrator's noise in close quarters; such a simple request for comfort. It broke my heart.

My sister lived a world away (a couple states and a thousand miles). She was really the only functioning adult relative I had. I brought her name up several times to Richard during our final years together. His response had always been negative with reasons why we didn't need to see them (Mary and her husband Darryl) or need their help. Male pride, I'm sure. But when I asked him, after the hospice duo and the air conditioning installers had all left, if I should call Mary and ask her to come and help, he said, "How soon can they be here?"

I was hyperventilating swallowing tears when I called Mary. I had located three homes that I wanted to go look at. A nurse friend had agreed to watch Rich while I checked them out. But then what? I needed help moving him and keeping myself together.

Mary and Darryl were there in eighteen hours in spite of driving a gas-guzzling truck and dragging a trailer behind them. Rich rallied. He tried his wheelchair in the middle of the kitchen while Mary and I fixed dinner. He wanted to see the new air-conditioning unit in the backyard. Darryl carried him over the gravel path. They perused the big square metal box with man-like interest. We decided against a tour of the new furnace. Darryl could not safely maneuver Rich down through the "Bat Cave" (what Rich and I called the steep narrow passage to the basement). Rich settled for my enthusiastic description of the easily-accessible slot where I would be changing the filters.

The weather had turned cool. "I thought I would get to use the air conditioning." Rich's disappointment flickered away. "But we got it for you."

It was our last day together at home. We were waiting for an extra-long hospital bed to be delivered to Helen's. The medications and oxygen units were already there. We had tried to say her name in Romanian but we just couldn't get the sounds right. She cringed at our attempts and said the English equivalent would be fine.

"Oh how good you look," Helen squealed when I wheeled Rich up the ramp to her back door just to take a look. She was lying. Only the day before my nurse friend who usually commented on Rich's "good color" whispered on her way out. "It won't be long, his color's not good." But Rich seemed to like Helen's compliment. We were there just to kick the tires so she wanted to make us feel welcome. Little did she know that she had almost no competition. Between room availability and Rich's request for a private bathroom, Helen was my best bet. The only other home in the running, although spacious, spotless and elegantly furnished, it lacked warmth. When we went (our second stop) to see it, the owner, a short man built like a rugby player stoically watched us drive up to his front yard.

"This is the guy who's goin' take care of me?" Rich wouldn't even get out of the car.

Rich actually ate some of what Mary fixed us for dinner. He was too exhausted to stay in the kitchen with us, so I fed it to him in bed. Our private times together were coming to an end; just a few more hours. I remember one detail; the sentence that

Rich could not finish without his voice breaking. The last two words I had to read on his lips because there was no sound, only tears. And all I had said was "I love you."

And all he said was, "More than. I could. *Ever. Know*."

I held Rich as close as I could. He knew I was not abandoning him. We were still on the carousel together. The music was softer; the lights dim. The turns were slower but I would be holding him until we coasted to a stop.

Although Rich enjoyed the flavors of Mary's dinner, the food did not settle well in his failing digestive system. Stomach rumblings brought an end to our quiet time. Rich was in a hurry. I rushed to get his clothes off but he hesitated at the commode. A crazy notion; he wanted to get to the bathroom. I was struggling, trying to keep him from lurching for the hall when it happened. The sound and the smell froze me. Rich's eyes were huge as I steadied him.

So, I guess this is what the hospice nurse *knew* was coming. I wondered what else would be happening as Rich's liver failed.

He finally spoke softly. "We gotta get me over to Helen's soon." We were both covered in poop.

With Mary's help, Richard, the room and I, all

got cleaned up. There was a terrifying near-slip in the shower. Many things had to be thrown away. I went to bed realizing how much worse it would have been if I had had to deal with it alone.

---

1. Adult foster care homes rent by the month.

The owner of the home may not want to rent to you if your loved one's life expectancy is less than 30 days. A partial reimbursement for days not used is not likely. However, it's a supply and demand business. It doesn't hurt to raise the possibility of pro-rated charges.

---

2. If you use a placement agency to find a home, there's no way you'll get a dime back.

The home pays most of the first month's rent to the placement agency. Adult foster care is state licensed, so lists of homes are publicly available if you have the time and the inclination to check them out on your own.

3. *Foster care rooms are mostly unfurnished.*

You can get medical equipment like hospital beds delivered, but other pieces of furniture like dressers, chairs, TV, favorite pillow will have to be brought from home.

4. *Adult foster care regulations differ from state to state and may not be available at all where you live.*

I never once regretted moving Richard to adult foster care. I am thankful that I was not within earshot of the agitation and confusion that filled his last days and nights.

Chapter Eighteen

THE WAY THE MUSIC STOPPED

Richard died ten days after I moved him out of our home. According to knowledgeable hospice staff, if a dying person wants you to be there when he dies, he will wait for you. However, if he wants to die alone, he will outwait you and all spectators. You may sit for hours, days even, but when you leave the room for a breath of air or a comfort call, you will miss it—that moment too personal to share.

I spent many hours wondering if Rich would wait for me. When he was at home, I knew I would be there. I had prepared myself for how it would be. A hospice volunteer would wait the death-watch with me. I had a book of the stages. Rich had actually gone through all the milestones more than once, but I expected to have some warning so that I could say good-bye. Somehow that seemed important to me.

There would be the phone call I would make to my sister who would relay the message to my parents and my niece. "They don't think Rich will make it through the night" or "He's taken a turn for the worse. We don't think he'll last much longer." Then I would have my quiet time with him where I could tell him how I love him and… something. I don't know what that something is because it didn't happen that way.

SEPTEMBER 9, 2008

Energized from my morning yoga class, I started talking to Rich as soon as I came into the room, running on about the joys of Namaste. They had him in a diaper, not the pull up pants I had brought with his clothes. The diaper made his hips look huge, like a clumsily-wrapped package with the catheter sticking out, taped to his scrawny thigh. The tubing ran over the side of his hospital bed into a plastic pouch of yellow liquid. His eyes were open but nothing else moved. They had given him a sponge bath. It was the first time he had been too weak to shower even seated in his wheelchair.

I continued my rapid-fire monologue as I moved to the foot of his bed to stand in his line of vision. A blanket made a tent over his feet that covered the bottom railing. I controlled an urge to touch to squeeze his feet. I wanted to hold them in my hands.

"Everybody's been so nice," I smiled, leveling my voice to cover the lump in my throat. I was running out of conversational material. "Siu Ling wants to adopt me. She's such a great neighbor. She told me anything I need, just to call her." I wondered if he could hear me. Maybe he had lost the ability to speak. His eyes appeared to be focused on me. Feeling lost, I stared at his motionless face, hoping for a smile. I waited, but he could not rise to the occasion. He could no longer rally his strength for my benefit. He could not smile for me. Then a new thought came to me. "And that new air-conditioning works great. I had it on last night."

The corners of his mouth moved up. I was so thrilled I reached out and squeezed his feet. There was no response. He looked uncomfortable. I rushed around to his bedside volunteering to adjust his pillows and I offered food, water. I suspended myself on straight forearms over him and kissed his forehead and his cheeks. I so wanted to wrap my arms around him and hold him tight.

His lips started to move. His Adam's apple made a strained movement. A weak whisper came out,

"Can I..." The movement of his mouth made a dry smacking sound in spite of the water I had just given him, "...just rest?"

I felt the chasm widening between us. On one side I was babbling about yoga and feeling good and he was dangling on the far side, suspended to life by a thread. I had been bothering him when he just wanted to sleep. I had been pestering him with everyday drivel when he was clutching the straws of consciousness. I whispered back hoping he understood me. "I'm sorry, sweetheart. I'll let you sleep."

I covered him up to his armpits, his bruised arms out of sight. He closed his eyes and I pulled a chair up next to him, resting my left hand on the lump that was his right hand. I sat calmly with him the way the hospice book instructed. I had read it so many times. He was supposed to know I was there, even if he didn't respond. I didn't need to do anything; just be normal and quiet... just *be* with him.

I turned the TV on so the sound was barely audible and watched the screen. There was baseball, the news channels. I watched and made quiet responsive sounds to the screen action, imagining us at home watching television together as we had for so many years. Tranquility turned into despair. The energy I had carried in with me had been sucked out. I wanted to go home and cry.

Stepping softly I checked his medication log. I scanned drawers for clean clothes, candy. I retrieved the last nicotine patch from the bureau. I fingered the smooth flat square and thought of the unopened box in the trunk of my car. Nicotine withdrawal seemed such a trivial, almost laughable, concern. "I'm going to put this last patch on," I whispered, thinking that I would return the unopened box to the store in the days to come. I lifted the bedspread from his arm and positioned the new dot just below the shadow of the old one. "I don't think you're goin' need any more of these, sweetheart."

His voice, that deep voice that I so loved, rang out above my whisper. As if we had been sitting at the kitchen table and I had asked if he wanted the rest of the meatloaf, he agreed quickly and loudly in spite of his eyes being closed. "Uh, huh." We were in agreement and he had heard everything I said.

I tossed the used patch and wrappings into the trash and went to tell Helen that I was leaving. I was saving my good-bye to Rich to be the last thing I did on my way out, but his snores kept me standing at the doorway of his room. His head arched back over his pillow, his mouth wide open, he snored deep rumbling sounds like I hadn't heard from him in a long time. I restrained myself from waking him with my needs. I would see him tomorrow. According to the nurse, we had at least two more weeks.

I cried all the way home. No matter how much longer his body would quiver and struggle to right itself, Rich was gone. The connection, the person who shared my world, had drifted away to a level just out of my reach. When I got home I peeled the "No Smoking—Oxygen in Use" signs off the doors. I called in-home services to pick up the back-up oxygen tank. Rich was never coming home.

I was up early the next morning. I had been self-talking myself into a positive attitude in the shower. When the phone rang at 8 AM I was toweling off.

"He's gone," is all Helen said.

"What do you mean he's gone?" I demanded. I was angry. He didn't wait for me. "You were supposed to tell me. So I could be there."

"Well, sometimes it happens like that." She offered no details.

I put down the phone. Abandoned. The carousel was dark and silent. I was standing alone on the platform. Richard had found his exit without me.

I learned later that day that it happened quickly; an ugly death. Ugly for me if I had seen it, but quick for him. Over the years as I retell what I know, I'm consoled that missing it was a blessing; the last gift Richard gave me. He let go. He was ready. I didn't need to see it.

Give your loved one permission to die.

I learned this critical lesson in the days after Rich's death. I learned it from his friend, Jeff, the friend who came around to visit with Rich through all those dying years. Other friends came once or twice, then never again. Not even a phone call. Not even to return Rich's calls. One friend came a few times to exchange books but the conversation was awkward although well-intentioned, with the warmth of a deposition.

Jeff came until the end. He took Rich out to lunch and coffee at the beginning. He sat in the backyard and shared stories when Rich became too weak for more. He visited him at the nursing home and his last days in foster care. He told stories and he listened.

I learned that Rich worried every day about what would happen to me. He fought death for over four years. He would not give up. He would not quit. I marveled at his tenacity. I had no idea he was holding on for me.

"He didn't want to leave you," Jeff said softly. "He was so worried about you. That's all he talked about. You were his whole world."

With this knowledge, I see my last afternoon with Richard as deep communication, my proof to him I was going to be all right. Unlike the doting caregiver that I had become for him, doing everything in my power to keep him alive, I showed joy to be alive without him. I had a good neighbor and others who would help me. When I quietly told Rich he wouldn't need any more nicotine patches, he trumpeted his agreement. We accepted the end together. There was no reason for him to stick around. I had given him permission to leave me. And within a few hours, he did.

I wish I had spoken the message to him earlier. I wish I had said in clear words that he could leave when he was ready and tired of fighting, that I was strong and that I would carry on. Why didn't I tell him he didn't have to prolong his suffering for my benefit? I didn't know he was. I didn't know my needs were part of his decision-making. He chose to endure treatments, procedures, medications that I would have passed on. Perhaps he would have too, if he had thought I was capable of surviving without him.

We knew the second cancer (liver cancer) would kill him. The oncologist said so the day he pronounced the diagnosis. It was only a matter of time. How Rich and I spent it was up to us. But the timing, when Rich would give up, that I left, unspoken, up to him. He didn't ask for my thoughts. I see now that he could have used my help with this task. Funny how we talked about everything but we did not talk about me letting him go.

Chapter Nineteen

TODAY... TOMORROW

Now that I have shared my story with you, I hope these slices from my life have been more than just a diversion. They were written to help you on your caregiving journey. Do you remember the five rules in the second chapter of this book? Do they create pictures in your mind? Can you see yourself acting them out? Let's review:

1. Remember that it's a marathon, not a sprint.

Caregiver days are long, so pace yourself. Take a look at your calendar. The days go on forever, each one full of routine and surprises. All the chores will be there every day. Pick only what you *can* do, then drop one out and add something for yourself.

Frantically shopping, cooking, zipping through traffic, thinking you will get ahead of the ever-increasing demands on you, only wears you out. You cannot afford to crash and burn.

---

2. *Train like an athlete.*

Your body and its ability to function reliably are more valuable than a multi-million-dollar NBA or MLB contract. At least two lives are depending on your continued performance, and one of them is yours. You need to be a well-oiled machine. Unlike professional sports, your season is open-ended. You don't know how long you'll be on the circuit. You are the star that determines the outcome of every game. Maintain your health. You know how to eat wholesome food, exercise, sleep right and stay hydrated. So, do it! You may not always be successful, but keep it as a priority. Do not ever dump this goal just because you think it's not helping. It is.

---

3. *Breathe, deeply, slowly, and often.*

Nourish your lungs continuously with oxygen.

Think of air as food your body needs more often than what you put in your stomach. Can you, right now, fill your lungs for ten seconds and hold your breath for ten seconds? Can you exhale slowly to a count of 10? 15? 20? Try it.

---

4. Nourish your spirit.

Replenish the energy that caregiving draws out of you every day. Take tiny pleasure breaks. Close your eyes and listen to a favorite song. Get lost in a magazine article or a game on your phone. Fantasize about what you would do if money were no object and you had all the time in the world.

---

5. Keep talking, working together to problem-solve.

You are not a paid stranger working a shift. You and your loved one are a team. You have handled other crises together before. If you cannot work as a team, get someone else to provide the care. It's fatal to you as a caregiver to try to do it alone in a hostile environment.

I have not gone into detail with these rules. It is not my intention to verse you in all phases of physical conditioning, spiritual energy and bed-side manner. There are scores of books written by experts to educate you in these areas. My desire is to show you, through my experiences, how important self-care is and to motivate you to explore and use these activities to enrich your caregiving life. If you have not yet formulated a goal for yourself, pick one of the above rules and see what it can do for you. There are excellent online resources to guide you.

My second goal for you, my caregiver audience, is to make you see and feel how important you are. You do what many people cannot. You are accomplishing something wonderful—lovingly taking care of someone very valuable to you. Do not let mind-numbing routine and insensitivity from others erode your self-esteem. Be proud.

May your baggage never be heavier than you can carry. May your caregiving days leave you with treasured memories and a new zest for life. One day soon this tremendous task you have, without hesitation, taken on will be complete and you will begin your new life with your new dreams . Let me be your role model. There *is* life after caregiving. Start planning yours now.

Footnote: *I did get to tango in my long black dress on a warm July evening in 2012. The night was magical, even if my escort was not. But that's a story for another time.*

Are you done with this book?

Please give it to a caregiver.

Don't know any?

Look around.

They are everywhere.
